AI Disclaimer

The information contained in this book is for educational and informational purposes only and should not be construed as financial advice. The cryptocurrency market is highly volatile and can involve significant risks. While every effort has been made to provide accurate and up-to-date information, the authors and publishers make no representations or warranties of any kind regarding the completeness, accuracy, reliability, or availability of the information contained in this book. Readers are encouraged to conduct their own research and consult with a qualified financial advisor before making any investment decisions. The authors and publishers shall not be liable for any losses or damages arising from the use of this book or reliance on the information provided herein. Investing in cryptocurrencies carries the risk of loss, and past performance is not indicative of future results. The strategies and insights presented in this book may not be suitable for all individuals. Always consider your financial situation, risk tolerance, and investment goals before engaging in cryptocurrency trading or investing. By reading this book, you acknowledge and accept these terms and agree that you will not hold the authors or publishers liable for any financial decisions made based on the content provided.

Table Of Contents

Chapter 2: Top Cryptocurrencies for 2025 2

Chapter 3: Emerging Cryptocurrencies with High Growth Potential. 2

Chapter 4: Sustainable and Eco-Friendly Cryptocurrencies 2

Chapter 5: DeFi Projects to Watch in 2025 2

Chapter 6: Cryptocurrency Investment Strategies for Beginners 2

Chapter 7: Risk Management Techniques in Cryptocurrency Trading 2

Chapter 8: Identifying Promising NFT Projects 2

Chapter 9: Analyzing Market Trends and Predictions for 2025 2

Chapter 10: Diversifying Your Crypto Portfolio 2

Chapter 11: Tax Implications and Strategies for Cryptocurrency Investors 2

Chapter 12: Long-Term vs. Short-Term Investment Strategies in Crypto 2

Chapter 13: Conclusion and Future Outlook 2

Chapter 1: Introduction to the Crypto Landscape in 2025 1

Chapter 1: Introduction to the Crypto Landscape in 2025

Overview of Cryptocurrency Trends

The landscape of cryptocurrency is continuously evolving, with trends emerging that can significantly impact investment strategies for both seasoned traders and newcomers alike. As we approach 2025, investors should closely monitor the increasing adoption of cryptocurrencies across various sectors, including finance, gaming, and supply chain management. This widespread acceptance is fueling the growth of established cryptocurrencies while simultaneously giving rise to innovative projects with high growth potential. Understanding these trends is crucial for investors looking to position themselves effectively in a rapidly changing market.

One key trend is the rise of decentralized finance (DeFi) projects, which are transforming traditional financial services by eliminating intermediaries and enabling peer-to-peer transactions. With the DeFi sector expected to expand significantly in 2025, investors should focus on identifying promising projects that offer unique value propositions. These may include lending platforms, decentralized exchanges, and yield farming opportunities. Engaging with these projects can provide substantial returns, but due diligence is essential to navigating the complexities of the DeFi ecosystem effectively.

Another significant trend is the growing emphasis on sustainable and eco-friendly cryptocurrencies. As environmental concerns gain traction, projects that prioritize energy efficiency and sustainability are becoming more attractive to ethical investors. In 2025, cryptocurrencies that utilize proof-of-stake mechanisms or other environmentally friendly consensus algorithms are likely to gain popularity. Investors should seek to diversify their portfolios by including these sustainable options, aligning their investments with broader ethical considerations while still pursuing financial growth.

The NFT market is also expected to continue its upward trajectory in 2025, with new applications and use cases emerging beyond digital art. Investors should keep an eye on promising NFT projects that tap into gaming, virtual real estate, and tokenized ownership. Understanding the nuances of NFT valuation and market dynamics will be crucial for investors looking to enter this space and capitalize on its growth potential. Additionally, integrating NFTs into a broader cryptocurrency strategy can enhance portfolio diversification and open avenues for unique investment opportunities.

Finally, effective risk management will remain a cornerstone of successful cryptocurrency trading in 2025. Given the inherent volatility of the market, investors should implement strategies that include setting stop-loss orders, diversifying holdings, and staying informed about market trends. By balancing long-term and short-term investment strategies, traders can navigate the complexities of the crypto landscape more successfully. As trends continue to shape the future of cryptocurrency, staying informed and adaptable will be essential for achieving investment success in this dynamic environment.

Importance of Strategic Investment

The importance of strategic investment in the cryptocurrency market cannot be overstated, especially as we approach 2025, a year anticipated to be pivotal for both established and emerging digital currencies. For cryptocurrency investors and day traders, the ability to navigate this volatile landscape requires a comprehensive understanding of market dynamics and the potential of various assets. Strategic investment goes beyond mere speculation; it involves meticulous planning, research, and adoption of various investment strategies tailored to individual risk tolerance and market conditions.

In 2025, the landscape of cryptocurrencies will likely feature a mix of established players and innovative newcomers. Investors must prioritize identifying top cryptocurrencies with strong fundamentals, technological advancements, and real-world applications. Emerging cryptocurrencies with high growth potential will be particularly attractive as they often represent the next wave of innovation in the crypto space. By strategically allocating resources to these promising assets, investors can position themselves to benefit from significant appreciation in value, making informed decisions based on thorough market analysis and trend examination.

Sustainability is another critical aspect of strategic investment in cryptocurrencies. As ethical investing gains traction, sustainable and eco-friendly cryptocurrencies are emerging as viable options for investors concerned with environmental impacts. Strategic investors will seek out projects that not only promise robust returns but also demonstrate a commitment to sustainability. This alignment of values and investment can enhance long-term profitability while appealing to a growing demographic of socially conscious investors.

Decentralized Finance (DeFi) projects represent yet another area of strategic investment that requires careful consideration. As the DeFi ecosystem continues to expand, investors must watch for projects that offer unique solutions to traditional financial challenges. Effective risk management techniques are essential for navigating the inherent volatility of these projects. Investors should focus on diversifying their portfolios, balancing risk across various asset classes, and employing strategies that mitigate potential losses while maximizing returns.

Ultimately, the success of any cryptocurrency investment hinges on a well-thought-out strategy that incorporates long-term and short-term investment goals. By analyzing market trends, understanding tax implications, and identifying promising NFT projects, investors can create a robust investment plan. The key to thriving in the crypto market lies in one's ability to adapt to changing conditions, remain informed, and make strategic decisions that align with both personal financial objectives and the broader market landscape.

Chapter 2: Top Cryptocurrencies for 2025

Bitcoin: The Digital Gold

Bitcoin has emerged as a pivotal asset in the cryptocurrency landscape, often referred to as "digital gold." As investors navigate the ever-evolving market of 2025, understanding Bitcoin's role and its potential for wealth preservation and growth is critical. Unlike traditional fiat currencies, Bitcoin operates on a decentralized network that enhances its security and reduces the risk of government manipulation. This unique attribute positions Bitcoin as a hedge against inflation, much like gold has historically provided, making it an essential component of any cryptocurrency investment strategy.

The characteristics that underpin Bitcoin's appeal as digital gold are its scarcity and divisibility. With a capped supply of 21 million coins, Bitcoin's scarcity creates an intrinsic value akin to precious metals. Investors are increasingly recognizing this, as Bitcoin's finite supply contrasts sharply with the unlimited printing of fiat currencies. Additionally, Bitcoin's divisibility allows for micro-investments, enabling both seasoned investors and newcomers to participate in the market. This accessibility broadens Bitcoin's appeal, helping it maintain its status as a foundational asset in cryptocurrency portfolios.

For cryptocurrency investors and day traders, the volatility of Bitcoin presents both opportunities and risks. The price fluctuations can be exploited for short-term gains, while long-term investors may choose to hold their assets during downturns, anticipating future appreciation. Incorporating Bitcoin into a diversified cryptocurrency portfolio can help balance risk and reward. By allocating a portion of their investments to Bitcoin, traders can leverage its historical price performance while mitigating the impact of downturns in other altcoins.

As the cryptocurrency market continues to mature, Bitcoin's role in decentralized finance (DeFi) cannot be overlooked. Numerous DeFi projects are emerging that utilize Bitcoin as collateral or incorporate it into their ecosystems. These innovations enhance Bitcoin's utility beyond a simple store of value, allowing for increased participation in lending, borrowing, and yield farming. Investors should keep an eye on these DeFi projects as they develop, as they may unlock additional value for Bitcoin holders and contribute to the overall growth of the cryptocurrency market.

Finally, understanding the tax implications of investing in Bitcoin is essential for maximizing returns. As regulations evolve, investors must be aware of how gains from Bitcoin trading are taxed in their jurisdictions. Proper tax planning can help minimize liabilities and ensure compliance. By employing sound risk management techniques, such as setting stop-loss orders and diversifying their portfolios, investors can navigate the complexities of the cryptocurrency market while capitalizing on Bitcoin's potential as a digital gold standard in 2025.

Ethereum: The Smart Contract Pioneer

Ethereum stands at the forefront of the cryptocurrency revolution as the leading platform for smart contracts, fundamentally transforming how transactions and agreements are executed online. Launched in 2015, Ethereum introduced a decentralized framework that allows developers to create and deploy applications without the need for intermediaries. This innovative technology has catalyzed the growth of decentralized finance (DeFi) and non-fungible tokens (NFTs), making it an essential asset for crypto investors to understand, especially as we approach 2025.

Smart contracts are self-executing contracts with the terms of the agreement directly written into code. This automation reduces the potential for fraud and enhances security, setting Ethereum apart from traditional contract mechanisms. As more industries recognize the benefits of smart contracts—ranging from finance to supply chain management—Ethereum's utility and demand are expected to grow significantly. For day traders and long-term investors alike, understanding the implications of this technology can lead to strategic advantages in a rapidly evolving market.

In 2025, the Ethereum platform is poised to continue its expansion, particularly with the ongoing development of Ethereum 2.0. This upgrade aims to improve scalability, security, and energy efficiency by transitioning from a proof-of-work to a proof-of-stake consensus mechanism. This shift not only addresses concerns about energy consumption—a critical factor for eco-conscious investors—but also positions Ethereum to support an increasing number of transactions without compromising speed or cost. As the ecosystem matures, identifying promising projects built on Ethereum can provide lucrative opportunities for both emerging and seasoned investors.

For investors focusing on DeFi, Ethereum remains the backbone of many innovative financial applications. Platforms offering lending, borrowing, and yield farming are flourishing, enabling users to maximize their returns without relying on traditional banks. As the DeFi space continues to mature, understanding the risks and rewards associated with these projects will be essential for effective investment strategies. Furthermore, with the rise of NFTs on the Ethereum blockchain, recognizing high-potential NFT projects can diversify portfolios and open new revenue streams for crypto enthusiasts.

As we progress through 2025, Ethereum will likely remain a staple in any well-rounded cryptocurrency portfolio. Its pioneering role in smart contracts coupled with robust ongoing development makes it a compelling choice for both short-term trading and long-term investment strategies. By analyzing market trends and leveraging risk management techniques, investors can navigate the complexities of the crypto landscape while positioning themselves to capitalize on Ethereum's continued growth and influence in the digital economy.

Binance Coin: Utility and Growth

Binance Coin (BNB) has emerged as a significant player in the cryptocurrency space, offering a blend of utility and growth that appeals to a wide range of investors. Originally created as a utility token for the Binance exchange, BNB has evolved into a versatile digital asset with a multitude of use cases. Investors can utilize BNB to pay for trading fees on the Binance platform at a discounted rate, which incentivizes its use among day traders looking to maximize their profits. In addition to trading fee discounts, BNB is also employed in various applications within the Binance ecosystem, including Binance Smart Chain (BSC), which supports decentralized applications (dApps) and DeFi projects.

The growth of Binance Coin is closely tied to the expansion of the Binance ecosystem itself. As one of the largest cryptocurrency exchanges globally, Binance has attracted millions of users, driving demand for BNB. The coin's integration into multiple platforms, such as Binance Launchpad for token sales and Binance Pay for merchant transactions, enhances its utility and positions it as a critical component of the burgeoning DeFi landscape. This utility not only fuels demand but also contributes to BNB's price appreciation, making it an attractive asset for investors eyeing high-growth potential in 2025.

Moreover, BNB is committed to sustainability, aligning with the interests of ethical investors. Binance has initiated programs aimed at reducing its carbon footprint, including investments in renewable energy projects. As the crypto market increasingly shifts towards sustainability, BNB's proactive approach to eco-friendliness can enhance its appeal to investors who prioritize ethical considerations in their portfolios. This focus on sustainability may also lead to increased adoption of BNB, as more projects and partnerships emerge that value environmentally conscious practices.

For those exploring investment strategies, BNB presents a unique opportunity for diversification. Its dual role as a utility token and a speculative asset allows investors to tailor their strategies based on market conditions. Day traders can capitalize on price volatility, while long-term investors may benefit from holding BNB as the Binance ecosystem continues to grow. Understanding market trends and incorporating BNB into a diversified portfolio can mitigate risk and enhance overall returns in the dynamic cryptocurrency landscape of 2025.

Finally, as cryptocurrency regulation becomes more prominent, understanding the tax implications of holding and trading BNB is essential for investors. The coin's growth trajectory, coupled with its diverse applications, necessitates a strategic approach to tax planning. Investors should stay informed about the evolving regulatory framework to effectively manage their portfolios and optimize returns. By leveraging the utility and growth potential of

Binance Coin, investors can position themselves advantageously within the competitive crypto market of 2025.

Cardano: The Sustainable Blockchain

Cardano has emerged as a leading player in the cryptocurrency landscape, particularly for those investors who prioritize sustainability and ethical investment strategies. Launched in 2017, Cardano distinguishes itself through its unique proof-of-stake consensus mechanism, which is significantly less energy-intensive compared to traditional proof-of-work systems. This environmentally friendly approach not only reduces the carbon footprint associated with blockchain operations but also aligns with a growing trend among investors who are increasingly concerned about the ecological implications of their investments. In 2025, as the global demand for sustainable solutions continues to rise, Cardano is well-positioned to attract a diverse range of investors seeking both ethical and profitable opportunities.

The scalability of Cardano's blockchain is another factor that makes it a compelling choice for cryptocurrency investors. Its layered architecture separates the settlement layer from the computation layer, allowing for greater flexibility and efficiency in processing transactions. This design enables Cardano to support a wide range of decentralized applications and smart contracts while maintaining high throughput and low transaction costs. As decentralized finance (DeFi) projects gain momentum, Cardano's ability to handle increased transaction volumes without compromising performance makes it a strong candidate for investors looking to capitalize on the DeFi boom in 2025.

In addition to its technical advantages, Cardano has cultivated a robust ecosystem of partnerships and community engagement that further enhances its credibility and growth potential. The platform has established collaborations with various governments and institutions to promote blockchain technology's adoption in real-world applications, particularly in regions where traditional financial systems are lacking. By focusing on practical use cases, Cardano not only enhances its value proposition but also creates opportunities for investors to participate in projects that can generate tangible benefits for communities, thereby promoting social impact alongside financial returns.

For cryptocurrency investors, understanding the risk management strategies associated with investing in Cardano is crucial. As with any digital asset, volatility remains a concern; however, Cardano's strong community support and continuous development mitigate some of these risks. Investors should consider diversifying their portfolios to include Cardano alongside other promising cryptocurrencies, balancing potential high-risk assets with more stable options. By adopting a prudent approach to risk management, investors can navigate the fluctuations of the crypto market while positioning themselves to take advantage of Cardano's long-term growth trajectory.

As the cryptocurrency landscape evolves, so too do the investment strategies that can lead to success. Cardano's focus on sustainability, combined with its innovative technological framework and community-driven initiatives, offers a unique opportunity for both novice and seasoned investors. By keeping an eye on market trends and embracing a diversified investment strategy, investors can position themselves strategically for the opportunities presented by Cardano and the broader cryptocurrency market in 2025. With its commitment to sustainability and ethical practices, Cardano not only represents a sound investment but also aligns with the values of an increasingly conscientious investor base.

Solana: Speed and Scalability

Solana has emerged as a formidable player in the cryptocurrency landscape, primarily due to its impressive speed and scalability. Designed to address the limitations faced by earlier blockchain networks, Solana boasts the ability to process thousands of transactions per second. This high throughput is achieved through a unique consensus mechanism called Proof of History, which allows the network to timestamp transactions and create a verifiable order of events without the need for extensive computational power. For cryptocurrency investors and day traders, this means that transactions can be executed quickly and reliably, making Solana an appealing option for those looking to capitalize on market opportunities.

One of the key factors contributing to Solana's success is its scalability. As more users and applications utilize the network, it can accommodate increased demand without sacrificing performance. This is particularly important in the context of decentralized finance (DeFi) and non-fungible tokens (NFTs), where high transaction volumes can often lead to slowdowns and increased fees on competing platforms. Solana's architecture supports a significant number of parallel transactions, ensuring that the network remains efficient even during peak usage times. This scalability positions Solana as a viable alternative for projects that require fast and low-cost transactions, which is a critical consideration for investors evaluating potential investments.

For ethical investors focused on sustainability, Solana presents an attractive option. Unlike some of its counterparts that rely on energy-intensive mining methods, Solana utilizes a more energy-efficient model. This aligns with the growing trend of eco-friendly cryptocurrencies, making it easier for investors to support projects that contribute positively to the environment while still providing robust investment opportunities. As the demand for sustainable investments rises, Solana's commitment to low energy consumption could enhance its appeal among socially conscious investors.

As we look ahead to 2025, the Solana ecosystem is poised for continued growth, with numerous DeFi projects and NFT marketplaces developing on its platform. Investors should closely monitor these emerging projects, as they can offer high growth potential and innovative solutions within the decentralized finance space. By staying informed about the latest developments and successfully identifying promising projects, investors can strategically position themselves to benefit from the anticipated expansion of the Solana network.

In terms of risk management, understanding Solana's unique attributes is crucial for both beginners and seasoned investors. The combination of speed, scalability, and sustainability makes Solana a compelling asset, but it is essential to remain vigilant about market trends and potential volatility. Diversifying a cryptocurrency portfolio with assets like Solana can help mitigate risks while maximizing potential returns. By incorporating Solana into a broader investment strategy, traders can take advantage of its strengths while balancing their exposure to other cryptocurrencies, ultimately leading to a more resilient investment approach in the dynamic crypto market of 2025.

Chapter 3: Emerging Cryptocurrencies with High Growth Potential

New Players in the Market

The cryptocurrency market continues to evolve rapidly, with new players emerging regularly. In 2025, several innovative projects are gaining attention, offering unique solutions and potential for substantial growth. These newcomers are often built on advanced technologies that enhance security, scalability, and efficiency, attracting both seasoned investors and newcomers to the space. As these projects enter the market, they provide opportunities for diversification, making it essential for investors to stay informed about these developments.

Among the most promising new entrants are those focused on sustainability and eco-friendliness. With increasing awareness of climate change and the environmental impact of traditional cryptocurrencies, several projects are positioning themselves as greener alternatives. These sustainable cryptocurrencies utilize energy-efficient consensus algorithms or leverage renewable energy sources to minimize their carbon footprint. For ethical investors, these options not only present potential financial returns but also align with their values, making them attractive in a market that increasingly values sustainability.

Decentralized Finance (DeFi) continues to be a driving force in the cryptocurrency sector, and new DeFi projects are emerging that offer innovative financial solutions. These projects provide services such as lending, borrowing, and yield farming without the need for traditional intermediaries. As the DeFi landscape expands, investors should pay close attention to new platforms that enhance user experience, improve security measures, and offer unique financial products. Understanding the intricacies of these DeFi projects can yield significant advantages, particularly for those looking to capitalize on the growing trend of decentralized financial services.

In addition to these developments, the NFT market is also evolving, with fresh concepts and platforms surfacing that promise to redefine digital ownership and creativity. New players are entering this space, creating unique ecosystems for artists, collectors, and investors. For those interested in identifying promising NFT projects, it is crucial to evaluate the underlying technology, community engagement, and the potential for real-world applications. The continued growth of NFTs indicates a lasting trend in the crypto market, making it an essential area for investors to explore.

As investors navigate this dynamic environment, employing effective investment strategies and risk management techniques becomes vital. Understanding the landscape of new players allows investors to make informed decisions, whether they are pursuing long-term growth or short-term gains. Diversifying a crypto portfolio to include these emerging cryptocurrencies can mitigate risks while maximizing potential returns. By remaining vigilant about market trends and adapting strategies accordingly, investors can position themselves advantageously in the ever-changing world of cryptocurrency.

Evaluating Projects: Key Indicators

Evaluating cryptocurrency projects requires a systematic approach focused on key indicators that can inform investment decisions. One of the primary indicators to assess is the project's utility and real-world application. A cryptocurrency that solves a genuine problem or fulfills a specific need is more likely to gain traction and achieve sustainable growth. Investors should analyze the use case presented by the project, looking for clear definitions of how the cryptocurrency will be utilized and the markets it aims to penetrate. Projects that demonstrate practical applications tend to attract user adoption, which is a critical factor for long-term success.

Another vital indicator is the team behind the project. The experience and background of the developers, advisors, and management can significantly influence a project's credibility and potential for success. Investors should conduct due diligence by researching the team's previous achievements in the crypto space or related industries. A transparent team with a solid reputation can instill confidence in potential investors, while a lack of information or a history of unsuccessful projects may signal red flags. Engaging with the community around the project can also provide insights into the team's responsiveness and commitment, which are crucial during challenging market conditions.

Market capitalization and trading volume are essential metrics that investors should analyze to understand a project's market standing. A higher market cap often indicates a more established and potentially stable investment, while trading volume can reveal the level of interest and liquidity in the market. Investors should look for projects that maintain healthy trading volumes, as this suggests active engagement and interest from the community. Additionally, examining historical price trends can help investors gauge volatility and overall market sentiment, aiding in the development of effective trading strategies.

The technology and security aspects of a project warrant careful evaluation as well. Investors should investigate the underlying blockchain technology, consensus mechanisms, and the project's approach to scalability and security. Projects that prioritize robust security measures and innovative technology are more likely to withstand market pressures and cyber threats. Furthermore, understanding the project's roadmap and upcoming milestones can provide insight into its growth potential and strategic direction. An ambitious yet realistic roadmap indicates a forward-thinking approach and a commitment to long-term development.

Lastly, the regulatory landscape surrounding the project is a crucial factor that can impact its viability. As governments around the world establish regulations for cryptocurrencies, projects that align with legal standards and adhere to compliance practices are more likely to thrive. Investors should stay informed about the regulatory environment in their jurisdictions and assess how potential changes could affect their investments. By keeping these key indicators in mind, cryptocurrency investors can make informed decisions, ultimately maximizing their chances of success in the evolving landscape of 2025.

Future-Proofing Your Investments

In the rapidly evolving landscape of cryptocurrency, future-proofing your investments requires a multifaceted approach that considers emerging trends, technological advancements, and market dynamics. As we look toward 2025, investors must be vigilant in identifying cryptocurrencies with high growth potential. This involves not only analyzing established currencies but also keeping an eye on new entrants that demonstrate innovative technology or strong use cases. Projects focused on scalability, interoperability, and real-world applications are particularly appealing, as they are more likely to gain traction in a competitive market.

Sustainable and eco-friendly cryptocurrencies have gained prominence, appealing to ethical investors who prioritize environmental considerations. As the world increasingly focuses on sustainability, cryptocurrencies that utilize energy-efficient consensus mechanisms or support green initiatives may offer a competitive edge. Investors should research projects that are committed to reducing their carbon footprints and promoting sustainability, ensuring that their portfolios align with their values while also tapping into a growing market segment.

Decentralized Finance (DeFi) projects are another key area for future-proofing investments. As traditional financial systems face disruption, DeFi platforms are gaining traction by providing innovative financial solutions that bypass intermediaries. Investors should keep abreast of emerging DeFi projects that offer unique services such as lending, staking, and yield farming. By diversifying into DeFi, investors can not only enhance their portfolios but also position themselves at the forefront of a financial revolution that is likely to reshape how assets are managed and exchanged.

Risk management is paramount in the volatile world of cryptocurrency trading. Investors must adopt comprehensive risk management techniques to protect their capital while maximizing potential returns. This includes setting stop-loss orders, diversifying across multiple cryptocurrencies, and conducting thorough research before making investment decisions. Understanding market trends and predictions for 2025 will also help investors make informed decisions, allowing them to anticipate shifts in market sentiment and adjust their strategies accordingly.

Lastly, tax implications and strategies play a crucial role in future-proofing cryptocurrency investments. As regulations evolve, it is essential for investors to stay informed about the tax obligations associated with their trading activities. Keeping detailed records of transactions, understanding the tax treatment of different assets, and consulting with tax professionals can help mitigate potential liabilities. By integrating tax planning into their investment strategies, investors can preserve their gains and ensure a more secure financial future in the ever-changing crypto landscape.

Chapter 4: Sustainable and Eco-Friendly Cryptocurrencies

The Rise of Green Cryptos

The rise of green cryptos represents a significant shift in the cryptocurrency landscape, driven by the urgent need for sustainable practices in the face of climate change. As awareness grows about the environmental impact of traditional cryptocurrencies, particularly those relying on energy-intensive mining processes, investors are increasingly drawn to alternatives that prioritize eco-friendliness. Green cryptos not only aim to reduce carbon footprints but also attract a new demographic of ethical investors looking to align their financial strategies with their values. This movement is reshaping market dynamics and influencing the investment choices of many, especially in the context of 2025.

Several cryptocurrencies have emerged as frontrunners in the green space, employing innovative technologies that promote sustainability. For instance, Proof of Stake (PoS) and other energy-efficient consensus mechanisms have gained traction, reducing energy consumption significantly compared to Proof of Work models. Projects like Cardano and Algorand are notable examples, as they prioritize eco-friendly operations without compromising on performance or scalability. Investors focused on long-term growth should consider these options, as they not only appeal to environmentally conscious users but also position themselves favorably with regulatory bodies increasingly concerned about sustainability.

In addition to established players, many new green crypto projects are entering the market, promising high growth potential in 2025. These emerging cryptocurrencies often focus on unique use cases that contribute positively to environmental outcomes, such as carbon credit trading or renewable energy financing. Investors should keep an eye on these innovative projects, as they not only offer the possibility of substantial returns but also contribute to a larger societal impact. Conducting thorough research into these projects, examining their technological foundations and real-world applications, is crucial for identifying the next big opportunities in the green crypto sector.

Decentralized Finance (DeFi) projects that incorporate sustainability into their frameworks are also gaining momentum. By leveraging smart contracts and blockchain technology, these projects allow users to engage in financial activities while supporting eco-friendly initiatives. DeFi platforms that reward users for staking or lending green cryptos can be particularly appealing to those looking to diversify their portfolios with sustainable assets. As the DeFi landscape continues to evolve, investors should evaluate which projects align with their financial goals while contributing positively to environmental efforts.

As with any investment, risk management techniques remain essential when venturing into the realm of green cryptos. While the potential for growth is significant, investors must also consider the volatility inherent in the cryptocurrency market. Diversifying portfolios to include a mix of traditional and green cryptos can help mitigate risks while capitalizing on emerging trends. Additionally, staying informed about regulatory developments and market trends is crucial for making educated investment decisions. By combining a sustainable approach with sound investment strategies, investors can navigate the green crypto landscape effectively and responsibly in 2025.

Evaluating Eco-Friendly Projects

Evaluating eco-friendly projects in the cryptocurrency space requires a thorough understanding of both the environmental implications of blockchain technology and the specific characteristics that define sustainable initiatives. As investors increasingly prioritize ethical considerations, recognizing projects that demonstrate a commitment to sustainability can offer significant advantages. To effectively evaluate these projects, investors should examine their energy consumption, consensus mechanisms, and overall impact on the environment. Projects utilizing proof-of-stake or other low-energy consensus algorithms typically present a more sustainable option compared to those relying on energy-intensive proof-of-work systems.

Another critical aspect of evaluating eco-friendly projects is assessing the transparency and authenticity of their sustainability claims. Investors should seek projects that provide clear data on their carbon footprint, energy sources, and initiatives aimed at minimizing environmental impact. Whitepapers, third-party audits, and sustainability reports can serve as valuable resources in this analysis. Engaging with the community and relying on feedback from environmentally-conscious investors can also offer insights into the project's credibility and integrity regarding its eco-friendly goals.

In addition to evaluating the environmental aspects, investors should consider the potential for growth and adoption of eco-friendly cryptocurrencies. The increasing global emphasis on sustainability and corporate responsibility suggests that projects focusing on eco-friendly solutions may experience heightened demand. Investors should analyze market trends, partnerships with environmentally focused organizations, and the overall market sentiment toward sustainability to gauge the future potential of these projects. Diversifying a portfolio with eco-friendly cryptocurrencies not only aligns with ethical investing but can also serve as a strategic move given the growing interest in sustainable finance.

Risk management is crucial when investing in eco-friendly projects. While the potential for growth is significant, the volatility of the cryptocurrency market can pose challenges. Investors should implement strategies to mitigate risks, such as setting stop-loss orders, conducting thorough research before investing, and not overcommitting resources to any single project. Understanding the unique challenges faced by eco-friendly initiatives, including regulatory scrutiny and technological barriers, can help investors better navigate the landscape and make informed decisions.

Finally, staying updated on regulations and policies impacting eco-friendly cryptocurrencies is essential for potential investors. As governments and institutions increasingly recognize the importance of sustainability, new regulations may emerge that could affect the viability and legality of certain projects. Investors should remain vigilant about changes in the regulatory environment, as these can significantly influence market dynamics and project success. By taking a comprehensive approach to evaluating eco-friendly projects, investors can position themselves advantageously in the evolving landscape of cryptocurrency investment, aligning their portfolios with both ethical considerations and potential high returns.

Investing with Ethics

Investing with ethics in the cryptocurrency space has become increasingly significant as more investors seek to align their financial goals with their personal values. In 2025, the landscape of ethical investing is shifting, with a growing emphasis on sustainable and eco-friendly cryptocurrencies. Investors are now more aware of the environmental impact of blockchain technologies, leading to a rising demand for projects that prioritize sustainability. Currencies such as Cardano and Algorand are gaining traction for their energy-efficient consensus mechanisms, making them appealing options for ethical investors looking to minimize their carbon footprint while maximizing returns.

DeFi projects are also at the forefront of ethical investment opportunities. These decentralized finance platforms promote financial inclusion by providing access to financial services for unbanked populations. By investing in DeFi projects that focus on community-driven initiatives, investors can contribute to a more equitable financial ecosystem. Projects like Aave and Uniswap not only enable users to lend and borrow assets but also emphasize transparency and decentralization, aligning with ethical investing principles. As the DeFi sector continues to grow, identifying projects that prioritize social good will be crucial for investors looking to make a positive impact.

For beginners entering the cryptocurrency market, understanding ethical investment strategies is essential. This includes conducting thorough research to identify projects that not only promise financial returns but also uphold ethical standards. Investors should consider the governance structures of these projects, looking for teams that prioritize community engagement and responsible management. Additionally, newcomers should be aware of the risks associated with investing in cryptocurrencies, including the volatility of the market and the potential for scams. By focusing on ethical practices and informed decision-making, beginner investors can navigate the complex crypto landscape more effectively.

Risk management techniques also play a vital role in ethical investing. Investors should implement strategies that protect their portfolios while adhering to their ethical commitments. This includes diversifying investments across a range of cryptocurrencies that meet ethical standards, thereby mitigating risk while supporting sustainable projects. Moreover, staying informed about market trends and regulatory developments is crucial for making educated investment choices. By blending ethical considerations with sound risk management practices, investors can achieve a balanced approach that aligns with their values.

As the cryptocurrency market evolves, the importance of investing with ethics will only continue to grow. Strategies that incorporate ethical considerations not only appeal to a broader audience of investors but also contribute to the development of a more sustainable and responsible financial ecosystem. As we look ahead to 2025, those who prioritize ethical investments will likely find themselves at the forefront of a movement that seeks to redefine the way we view and engage with cryptocurrencies. By fostering a culture of ethical investing, the crypto community can build a future that reflects both financial ambition and social responsibility.

Chapter 5: DeFi Projects to Watch in 2025

Understanding Decentralized Finance

Decentralized Finance, commonly referred to as DeFi, represents a transformative shift in the financial landscape, enabling peer-to-peer financial transactions without the need for traditional intermediaries such as banks. At its core, DeFi leverages blockchain technology to create open-source protocols that allow users to lend, borrow, trade, and invest in cryptocurrencies and digital assets. This shift is particularly appealing to cryptocurrency investors and day traders, as it provides opportunities to engage in yield farming, liquidity mining, and decentralized exchanges that often offer greater returns than traditional financial systems.

For investors looking to capitalize on emerging cryptocurrencies with high growth potential in 2025, DeFi projects should be a focal point. These projects often introduce innovative financial products and services, creating new markets and investment avenues. For instance, platforms that enable automated market-making or those that allow users to stake their assets for rewards are gaining traction. By closely monitoring the development of these projects and understanding their underlying technology, investors can identify which DeFi tokens have the potential to appreciate significantly in value.

Sustainability is increasingly becoming a priority for ethical investors, and the DeFi space is no exception. Many DeFi protocols are now incorporating eco-friendly practices, such as using energy-efficient consensus mechanisms or funding projects aimed at reducing carbon footprints. As the demand for sustainable investment options grows, investors should be aware of which DeFi projects align with these values. This not only positions them favorably within an ethical investment landscape but also taps into a burgeoning market trend that could yield high returns.

Risk management is paramount in cryptocurrency trading, particularly in the volatile DeFi sector. Investors must develop strategies that account for the unique risks associated with decentralized platforms, such as smart contract vulnerabilities, liquidity risks, and market fluctuations. Implementing stop-loss orders, diversifying investments across multiple DeFi projects, and regularly reassessing the market can help mitigate potential losses. Furthermore, understanding the mechanics of each DeFi protocol can aid in making informed decisions and establishing a robust risk management framework.

As the DeFi ecosystem continues to evolve, identifying promising NFT projects also becomes crucial for investors looking to diversify their portfolios. Many DeFi platforms are integrating NFTs, creating unique financial products that combine the benefits of digital art and collectibles with the liquidity and accessibility of decentralized finance. By analyzing market trends and predictions for 2025, investors can pinpoint which NFT projects are likely to succeed and how they can complement their DeFi investments, ultimately leading to a more balanced and potentially lucrative cryptocurrency portfolio.

Top DeFi Platforms and Protocols

Decentralized Finance (DeFi) has emerged as one of the most revolutionary sectors within the cryptocurrency landscape, offering a plethora of opportunities for investors and traders alike. As we approach 2025, understanding the leading DeFi platforms and protocols is essential for anyone looking to capitalize on this burgeoning market. These platforms facilitate various financial services, such as lending, borrowing, trading, and yield farming, without the need for traditional intermediaries. By leveraging blockchain technology, they provide users with greater control over their assets and the potential for higher returns, all while minimizing friction and costs associated with traditional finance.

Among the top DeFi platforms, Ethereum remains the backbone of the DeFi ecosystem. Its robust infrastructure supports a multitude of protocols, including Uniswap, Aave, and Compound. Uniswap, a decentralized exchange, allows users to swap various cryptocurrencies without relying on a central authority, offering liquidity pools that reward users for providing liquidity. Aave and Compound, on the other hand, are lending protocols that enable users to earn interest on their cryptocurrency holdings or borrow assets against their collateral. As Ethereum continues to evolve, with upgrades aimed at improving scalability and reducing transaction costs, these platforms are likely to enhance their offerings and attract even more users.

Another notable contender in the DeFi space is Binance Smart Chain (BSC), which has gained traction due to its lower fees and faster transaction speeds compared to Ethereum. Platforms like PancakeSwap and Venus have gained significant popularity among investors looking for alternatives to Ethereum-based projects. PancakeSwap functions similarly to Uniswap but operates on the BSC network, providing users with a seamless trading experience. Venus combines lending and stablecoin minting, allowing users to leverage their assets while maintaining liquidity. As more projects migrate to BSC, this ecosystem will likely continue to grow, offering diverse opportunities for savvy investors.

For those focused on sustainable and eco-friendly investments, DeFi projects that align with these values are emerging. Protocols such as Algorand and Tezos not only prioritize scalability and efficiency but also emphasize environmental sustainability. Algorand's consensus mechanism is designed to be energy-efficient, making it an attractive option for ethical investors. Similarly, Tezos employs a proof-of-stake mechanism that reduces energy consumption significantly compared to traditional proof-of-work systems. Investing in these platforms not only supports innovative financial solutions but also aligns with a growing demand for responsible investing practices.

As the DeFi landscape evolves, risk management remains a critical consideration for investors. Understanding the underlying protocols, assessing their security measures, and diversifying across multiple platforms can help mitigate potential losses. Engaging in thorough research and utilizing tools to monitor market trends will equip investors with the necessary insights to navigate this dynamic space. With the right strategies in place, the top DeFi platforms and protocols can serve as powerful vehicles for achieving financial goals in the ever-expanding world of cryptocurrency.

Risks and Rewards in DeFi

Risks and rewards in decentralized finance (DeFi) are critical considerations for any cryptocurrency investor or day trader looking to navigate this rapidly evolving landscape in 2025. DeFi offers the promise of innovative financial services without the intermediaries typically found in traditional finance. However, the potential for high returns comes with significant risks, including smart contract vulnerabilities, market volatility, and regulatory uncertainties. Investors must be aware of these factors to make informed decisions about their involvement in DeFi projects.

One of the primary rewards of engaging with DeFi is the opportunity for yield farming and liquidity provision, which can generate substantial passive income. By providing liquidity to decentralized exchanges or lending platforms, investors can earn rewards in the form of interest or token incentives. These opportunities often yield returns that surpass those available through traditional banking systems, making them attractive for those willing to embrace the associated risks. However, the potential for high returns also means that investors should conduct thorough research to identify sustainable projects with solid fundamentals.

On the flip side, the risks inherent in DeFi are amplified by the nascent nature of the technology and the rapid pace of innovation. Smart contracts, which automate transactions and protocols, can contain bugs or vulnerabilities that hackers may exploit, leading to significant financial losses. Additionally, the lack of regulatory oversight can expose investors to scams and fraudulent projects. Understanding these risks is crucial for developing effective risk management techniques, such as diversifying your portfolio across various DeFi projects and employing stop-loss orders to mitigate potential losses.

Regulatory risks also loom large in the DeFi space, as governments around the world grapple with how to approach cryptocurrencies and decentralized financial systems. The evolving regulatory landscape can impact the viability and legality of certain DeFi projects, making it essential for investors to stay informed about changes that could affect their investments. Engaging with projects that prioritize compliance and transparency can help reduce exposure to regulatory risks, ensuring that investments remain viable in the long term.

In conclusion, navigating the risks and rewards in DeFi requires a balanced approach and a willingness to adapt to changing market conditions. Investors should focus on thorough research, understanding the underlying technology, and staying updated on regulatory developments. By employing sound risk management strategies and diversifying their portfolios, cryptocurrency investors can position themselves to capitalize on the exciting opportunities that DeFi presents while minimizing potential downsides. This informed approach will be crucial for successfully navigating the DeFi landscape in 2025 and beyond.

Chapter 6: Cryptocurrency Investment Strategies for Beginners

Getting Started: First Steps

Getting started in the world of cryptocurrency can be both exciting and daunting, especially as we approach the pivotal year of 2025. For investors and day traders alike, the first steps are crucial in establishing a solid foundation for your investment journey. Begin by educating yourself about the different types of cryptocurrencies available, focusing on the top currencies that are projected to perform well in 2025. Familiarizing yourself with established coins like Bitcoin and Ethereum, as well as emerging cryptocurrencies that show high growth potential, will provide a sturdy base for your investment strategy.

Once you have a grasp of the landscape, it's essential to choose the right platforms for buying and trading cryptocurrencies. Selecting reputable exchanges that offer a wide variety of coins, along with robust security measures, will enhance your trading experience. Additionally, consider the user interface and transaction fees associated with these platforms. Many traders find it beneficial to use multiple exchanges to take advantage of differing prices and liquidity levels across the market, which can lead to better trading opportunities.

As you begin to build your portfolio, think about diversifying your investments. This strategy is crucial in managing risk and maximizing returns. Look into sustainable and eco-friendly cryptocurrencies that appeal to ethical investors, as these are gaining traction and may offer unique investment opportunities. Simultaneously, keep an eye on DeFi projects that are making waves in the financial sector. Understanding the principles behind these projects will help you identify those with the most potential for growth.

Risk management is vital in the volatile world of cryptocurrency trading. Establish clear guidelines for how much capital you are willing to allocate to each investment and set stop-loss orders to protect your assets. Additionally, develop a strategy that outlines your long-term versus short-term investment goals. This dual approach allows you to capture immediate gains while securing positions in promising projects for the long haul, striking a balance that can lead to sustained profitability.

Finally, stay informed about market trends and predictions for 2025, as these insights can significantly influence your investment decisions. Analyze market reports, follow influential figures in the crypto space, and engage with communities to gather diverse perspectives. Understanding tax implications and strategies for cryptocurrency investments is also crucial, as this knowledge will help you navigate potential pitfalls. By taking these first steps with diligence and a strategic mindset, you can position yourself for success in the dynamic and evolving world of cryptocurrency investing.

Basic Investment Strategies

Investing in cryptocurrencies requires a sound understanding of various strategies that can help maximize returns while managing risks. A fundamental approach is to distinguish between short-term and long-term investment strategies. Short-term trading, often favored by day traders, involves taking advantage of price volatility to realize gains quickly. This strategy requires a keen eye for market trends and often relies on technical analysis to make informed decisions. In contrast, long-term investing focuses on the potential for significant appreciation over time, allowing investors to benefit from the overall growth of the cryptocurrency market, especially in promising projects that are expected to mature in the coming years.

Emerging cryptocurrencies represent another vital area of focus for investors seeking high growth potential in 2025. Identifying these opportunities often involves thorough research into new projects, their use cases, the team behind them, and their community support. Investors should look for projects that solve real-world problems and have unique selling propositions. Engaging with online communities, following industry news, and analyzing whitepapers can provide insights into which emerging coins might become the next big players in the crypto landscape. As the market evolves, being early to invest in these cryptocurrencies can lead to substantial returns.

Sustainable and eco-friendly cryptocurrencies are gaining traction, appealing to ethical investors. As concerns about the environmental impact of cryptocurrency mining grow, projects that prioritize sustainability will likely attract more attention and investment in 2025. Investors should consider cryptocurrencies that utilize energy-efficient consensus mechanisms or those that contribute positively to environmental sustainability. By aligning investment choices with personal values, investors can participate in the crypto market while promoting responsible practices, ensuring that their portfolios reflect their ethical considerations.

DeFi projects are revolutionizing traditional finance, offering a plethora of investment opportunities. Investors should keep a close eye on promising DeFi platforms in 2025, as they provide innovative solutions such as lending, borrowing, and yield farming. Understanding the unique features and risks associated with each DeFi project is crucial. Effective risk management techniques, such as diversifying investments across various DeFi platforms and using stop-loss orders, can help mitigate potential losses. Investors should also stay informed about regulatory changes affecting DeFi, as these can impact project viability and profitability.

Finally, diversification remains a cornerstone of effective cryptocurrency investment strategies. By spreading investments across different asset classes, including established cryptocurrencies, emerging projects, and DeFi tokens, investors can reduce risk and enhance potential returns. Additionally, monitoring market trends and adjusting portfolios in response to shifts in the crypto landscape is essential for long-term success. Understanding tax implications and developing strategies to optimize tax responsibilities can further improve overall investment outcomes. By adopting a comprehensive approach that combines these basic investment strategies, investors can position themselves for success in the dynamic world of cryptocurrencies in 2025.

Building Confidence in Trading

Building confidence in trading is essential for anyone venturing into the dynamic world of cryptocurrencies. As the market continues to evolve, understanding the fundamentals of trading and investing becomes increasingly important. For cryptocurrency investors and day traders, confidence stems from a combination of knowledge, experience, and a well-structured approach. By focusing on the top cryptocurrencies and developing effective strategies, investors can navigate the complexities of the market with greater assurance.

One of the first steps to building confidence in trading is education. Investors should familiarize themselves with various cryptocurrencies, especially those projected to have high growth potential in 2025. This includes researching emerging cryptocurrencies that are gaining traction and understanding their underlying technologies and use cases. Knowledge empowers investors to make informed decisions, reducing the fear and uncertainty often associated with trading. Additionally, staying updated on market trends and predictions for 2025 will help traders identify promising opportunities and avoid pitfalls.

Risk management is another critical aspect of building confidence in trading. Understanding the inherent risks in the cryptocurrency market and implementing effective risk management techniques can significantly enhance an investor's confidence. This includes setting stop-loss orders, diversifying portfolios, and only investing what one can afford to lose. By clearly defining risk thresholds and adhering to them, traders can mitigate emotional reactions during market fluctuations, leading to more rational decision-making.

Furthermore, developing a solid trading strategy tailored to individual goals can bolster confidence. Whether an investor is focused on long-term gains or short-term profits, having a defined strategy helps guide trading actions and reduces impulsive decisions. For beginners, adopting straightforward strategies and gradually refining them as experience grows can pave the way for success. Engaging with DeFi projects or exploring sustainable cryptocurrencies can also align trading strategies with personal values, enhancing overall confidence in investments.

Lastly, community engagement and networking play a pivotal role in building confidence. By connecting with other traders and investors through forums, social media, and local meetups, individuals can share experiences, insights, and strategies. Learning from others who have faced similar challenges can provide valuable perspectives and encouragement. As investors share in the successes and failures of their peers, they can foster a supportive environment that bolsters collective confidence in navigating the ever-evolving landscape of cryptocurrency trading.

Chapter 7: Risk Management Techniques in Cryptocurrency Trading

Identifying Risks in Crypto Investments

Identifying risks in crypto investments is a crucial step for any investor looking to navigate the volatile landscape of digital currencies. The first area of concern is market volatility, which can lead to significant fluctuations in asset values. Prices of cryptocurrencies can swing widely within short periods, driven by factors such as market sentiment, regulatory news, and macroeconomic trends. Investors need to be prepared for the possibility of sudden downturns and should consider implementing stop-loss orders or other risk mitigation strategies to protect their capital.

Another critical risk to consider is the regulatory environment surrounding cryptocurrencies. Governments around the world are still determining how to regulate digital assets, and changes in regulation can have immediate and profound effects on the market. Investors must stay informed about regulatory developments in their jurisdictions and globally, as new laws or restrictions can impact the liquidity and viability of certain cryptocurrencies. Engaging with communities and following reputable news sources can help investors anticipate changes and adjust their strategies accordingly.

Security risks also pose a significant threat to crypto investments. Unlike traditional financial systems, which have established protections in place, the decentralized nature of cryptocurrencies means that investors must take personal responsibility for securing their assets. Hacks and scams are prevalent in the crypto space, so employing best practices such as using hardware wallets, enabling two-factor authentication, and remaining vigilant against phishing attempts is essential. Understanding the risks associated with different platforms and protocols can help investors make informed decisions about where to store and trade their cryptocurrencies.

Liquidity risk is another important factor to consider when investing in cryptocurrencies. Some digital assets may have low trading volumes, making it difficult to buy or sell them without affecting the market price. This can be particularly relevant for emerging cryptocurrencies with high growth potential. Investors should assess the liquidity of a cryptocurrency before making significant investments, ensuring that they can enter and exit positions with minimal price impact. Analyzing market depth and volume can provide insights into the liquidity of a particular asset.

Lastly, the risk of technological failure should not be overlooked. The underlying technology of cryptocurrencies, including blockchain networks and smart contracts, can be susceptible to bugs, vulnerabilities, or even catastrophic failures. As the space evolves, new projects may emerge with innovative technologies, but they can also come with unknown risks. Investors should conduct thorough due diligence on the technological foundations of the cryptocurrencies they are considering, evaluating the development teams, project roadmaps, and community support to gauge their long-term viability. Taking these risks into account will help investors build a more robust and strategically sound crypto portfolio.

Tools and Techniques for Risk Mitigation

Risk mitigation is a critical aspect of successful cryptocurrency investing, especially for those navigating the volatile markets of 2025. Investors must equip themselves with a set of tools and techniques designed to minimize risks while maximizing potential returns. One fundamental approach to risk management is the use of stop-loss orders. These orders allow traders to set predefined exit points for their investments, automatically selling assets when prices fall below a certain threshold. This technique helps to limit losses and protect capital, ensuring that investors can stay in the game even during turbulent market conditions.

Another effective risk mitigation strategy is portfolio diversification. By spreading investments across various cryptocurrencies, including emerging projects with high growth potential and sustainable coins, investors can reduce the impact of a poor-performing asset on their overall portfolio. This strategy not only includes diversifying across different cryptocurrencies but also considering different sectors within the crypto space, such as DeFi projects or promising NFT platforms. By doing so, investors can balance their exposure to risk while taking advantage of the unique opportunities that each sector presents.

In addition to diversification, regular market analysis is essential for informed decision-making. Investors should utilize various analytical tools and techniques to track market trends, identify potential red flags, and capitalize on emerging opportunities. This can include technical analysis, which involves studying price charts and indicators, as well as fundamental analysis, which evaluates the underlying value of a cryptocurrency based on its technology, use case, and team. By combining these analytical methods, investors can gain deeper insights into market movements and make more strategic investment choices.

Furthermore, staying informed about regulatory developments and tax implications is crucial for risk management in cryptocurrency investing. As governments around the world continue to shape the legal landscape for digital currencies, understanding how these regulations affect investments can help investors avoid costly pitfalls. Additionally, implementing tax-efficient strategies can enhance overall profitability. Investors should consider consulting with tax professionals who are well-versed in cryptocurrency to ensure compliance and optimize their investment outcomes.

Lastly, continuous education and adaptation are vital in the fast-evolving crypto landscape. Investors should engage with educational resources, attend industry seminars, and participate in online forums to enhance their understanding of market dynamics and risk management techniques. As new technologies and trends emerge, being proactive and adaptable will allow investors to refine their strategies and effectively mitigate risks. By employing these tools and techniques, crypto investors can navigate the complexities of the market and position themselves for success in 2025 and beyond.

Developing a Risk Management Plan

Developing a comprehensive risk management plan is essential for any investor navigating the volatile landscape of cryptocurrencies. With the rapid evolution of digital currencies, particularly in 2025, investors must adopt a proactive approach to mitigate potential losses while maximizing their chances of success. A well-structured risk management plan involves several key components, including risk identification, risk assessment, risk control, and monitoring. Each of these elements plays a crucial role in ensuring that investors can maintain their positions even in the face of market fluctuations.

The first step in developing a risk management plan is to identify the specific risks associated with cryptocurrency investments. These risks can range from market volatility and technological vulnerabilities to regulatory changes and liquidity issues. Market volatility is particularly pronounced in the crypto space, where prices can swing dramatically within short time frames. Additionally, the emergence of new cryptocurrencies and DeFi projects introduces further uncertainty. By pinpointing these risks, investors can create strategies tailored to their unique situations and investment goals.

Once risks have been identified, the next phase involves assessing their potential impact on the investment portfolio. This assessment requires investors to analyze historical data, market trends, and current economic conditions. For instance, understanding how certain cryptocurrencies responded to past market downturns can provide valuable insights into potential future performance. Investors should also consider their own risk tolerance levels, which can vary based on individual financial situations and investment objectives. This combination of quantitative analysis and personal assessment will help guide informed decision-making.

The implementation of risk control measures is a critical aspect of any risk management plan. Investors can employ various techniques, such as setting stop-loss orders, diversifying their portfolios across multiple cryptocurrencies, and limiting the size of individual positions. Additionally, staying updated on market news and technological advancements can help investors anticipate potential risks and react swiftly. By adopting these strategies, investors can better protect their capital and enhance their potential for returns, particularly in a landscape where new opportunities and challenges continually arise.

Finally, continuous monitoring and review of the risk management plan are vital for long-term success. The cryptocurrency market is dynamic, with new trends and regulatory developments emerging regularly. Investors should routinely assess the effectiveness of their risk management strategies and make adjustments as necessary. This ongoing evaluation not only ensures that the plan remains relevant but also helps investors stay ahead of the curve in 2025's rapidly changing crypto environment. By committing to a robust risk management approach, cryptocurrency investors can navigate the complexities of the market with greater confidence and resilience.

Chapter 8: Identifying Promising NFT Projects

Understanding NFTs and Their Value

Non-fungible tokens (NFTs) have emerged as a revolutionary segment within the cryptocurrency landscape, drawing significant interest from investors, collectors, and creators alike. Unlike traditional cryptocurrencies such as Bitcoin or Ethereum, which are fungible and can be exchanged on a one-to-one basis, NFTs represent unique digital assets. This uniqueness is what gives NFTs their value, as they can represent ownership of a wide range of digital items, including art, music, virtual real estate, and even tweets. The distinctive nature of NFTs makes them particularly appealing in a digital economy increasingly focused on rarity and provenance.

The value of an NFT is determined by several factors, including its scarcity, the reputation of the creator, and the demand within the market. Scarcity can be artificially created by limiting the number of tokens issued for a particular item or by establishing a unique piece that cannot be duplicated. The creator's brand or track record plays a vital role in influencing an NFT's value; works by renowned artists or influencers often command higher prices due to their established reputations. Additionally, market demand fluctuates based on trends, cultural significance, and the overall sentiment within the cryptocurrency community, making it essential for investors to stay informed about these dynamics.

Investing in NFTs requires a different strategy compared to traditional cryptocurrencies. While many investors focus on established currencies for their relative stability, NFTs can be more volatile and subject to rapid price changes based on trends and public perception. For day traders and cryptocurrency investors, it is crucial to identify promising NFT projects that exhibit potential for growth. This can involve researching upcoming artists, exploring innovative platforms, and analyzing market trends to determine which NFTs might appreciate in value. Tools like social media sentiment analysis and market tracking platforms can assist investors in making informed decisions.

As with any investment, risk management is vital when dealing with NFTs. The NFT market can be unpredictable, with prices that can surge or plummet based on market sentiment or external factors. Diversification remains a key strategy; investors should consider spreading their investments across different NFT categories, such as art, gaming, and virtual real estate, to mitigate risks. Furthermore, understanding the tax implications of buying and selling NFTs is essential, as regulations continue to evolve. Keeping comprehensive records of transactions and understanding local laws can aid in navigating tax responsibilities effectively.

In conclusion, while NFTs present lucrative opportunities for investors in 2025, understanding their unique value proposition is critical for success. Recognizing the factors that contribute to the worth of NFTs, employing effective investment strategies, and managing risks will be essential for those looking to capitalize on this emerging asset class. As the crypto landscape continues to evolve, staying ahead of market trends and being adaptable will be key for both new and experienced investors in navigating this exciting frontier.

Market Trends in NFTs

Market trends in NFTs are evolving rapidly, reflecting broader shifts within the cryptocurrency landscape. As 2025 approaches, the NFT market is poised for significant growth, driven by technological advancements, increased mainstream adoption, and evolving consumer preferences. Investors are increasingly recognizing NFTs not just as digital collectibles, but as integral components of broader investment strategies. The convergence of NFTs with various sectors, such as gaming, art, and real estate, is reshaping how these digital assets are perceived and valued.

One prominent trend is the rise of utility-based NFTs. Unlike traditional NFTs that primarily serve as collectibles, utility NFTs provide tangible benefits to holders, such as access to exclusive events, services, or content. This shift is attracting a wider audience, including those who may not consider themselves traditional collectors. Investors should pay attention to projects that emphasize functionality and community engagement, as these attributes are likely to drive demand and increase long-term value.

Another significant trend is the integration of NFTs with decentralized finance (DeFi) platforms. As DeFi continues to disrupt traditional finance, NFTs are finding new roles within this ecosystem. For instance, NFTs can be used as collateral for loans, enabling holders to leverage their digital assets without liquidating them. This innovative intersection of NFTs and DeFi presents unique opportunities for investment, allowing traders to maximize their returns while minimizing risks. Keeping an eye on projects that blend these two sectors can reveal promising investment avenues.

Sustainability is becoming increasingly important in the NFT space, with eco-friendly projects gaining traction among ethical investors. As concerns about the environmental impact of blockchain technologies grow, initiatives that prioritize sustainable practices are emerging. NFTs built on energy-efficient blockchains or those that incorporate carbon offsetting strategies are likely to attract a dedicated investor base. This trend highlights the importance of aligning investment choices with personal values, particularly for those looking to make a positive impact through their financial decisions.

Finally, market predictions for 2025 suggest that the NFT landscape will continue to diversify, with a focus on innovation and integration with other technologies. As new use cases for NFTs are discovered, such as in identity verification and supply chain management, the potential for growth is substantial. Investors should remain vigilant in identifying promising NFT projects that demonstrate real-world applications and scalability. By understanding these market trends, investors can better position themselves to capitalize on the NFT boom and make informed decisions in the rapidly changing crypto environment.

Tips for Spotting Successful NFT Projects

When seeking to identify successful NFT projects, investors should begin by examining the underlying utility of the token. Projects that offer tangible benefits, such as access to exclusive content, community engagement, or unique experiences, are typically more sustainable in the long run. For instance, NFTs that grant holders rights to physical assets, memberships, or services provide a stronger incentive for buyers beyond mere speculation. Understanding the value proposition of an NFT can help differentiate between projects that are likely to thrive and those that may fizzle out.

Another critical factor to consider is the team behind the NFT project. A strong, experienced team with a proven track record in the blockchain or entertainment industry can significantly enhance a project's credibility. Investors should look for transparency in the team's background, their previous successes, and their engagement with the community. Projects with active and responsive teams tend to foster better relationships with their supporters, which can lead to a more robust and loyal user base.

Community involvement and engagement are also crucial indicators of a project's potential success. A thriving community not only drives interest but also promotes organic growth through word-of-mouth. Investors should assess the project's social media presence, forums, and other communication channels to gauge community sentiment. Projects with active discussions, collaborations, and events tend to build stronger networks, which can be a significant asset in a competitive market.

Market trends should not be overlooked when evaluating NFT projects. Investors should analyze current trends in the broader NFT space, such as shifts toward specific types of art, gaming, or virtual real estate. Keeping an eye on emerging genres and popular platforms can provide insights into where the market is headed. Additionally, monitoring sales data and trading volumes can offer clues about the project's market traction and potential longevity.

Finally, due diligence is paramount. Investors should conduct thorough research, including reading whitepapers, understanding the project's roadmap, and assessing the overall market sentiment. Engaging with existing holders and seeking feedback can provide valuable insights. By combining qualitative assessments with quantitative data, investors can make informed decisions, ultimately increasing their chances of identifying successful NFT projects that align with their investment strategies in 2025.

Chapter 9: Analyzing Market Trends and Predictions for 2025

Historical Market Trends

In the ever-evolving landscape of cryptocurrency, historical market trends provide invaluable insights for investors and traders navigating the complexities of this digital frontier. Analyzing past performance patterns enables market participants to identify potential opportunities and pitfalls, especially as they prepare for the unique dynamics of 2025. The cryptocurrency market has experienced significant volatility, characterized by sharp price surges followed by steep declines. Understanding these fluctuations is crucial for developing effective investment strategies that cater to both short-term traders and long-term holders.

One notable trend observed in the cryptocurrency market is the increasing correlation between major cryptocurrencies such as Bitcoin and Ethereum with traditional financial markets. This relationship suggests that macroeconomic factors, including inflation rates and interest rates, are beginning to influence crypto prices more significantly. As investors become more aware of these correlations, they can better position their portfolios to hedge against market downturns or capitalize on upward trends. This understanding will be essential for anyone looking to make informed decisions in 2025, particularly as the global economy continues to recover from recent disruptions.

Emerging cryptocurrencies have also demonstrated the potential for explosive growth, often following the patterns established by their predecessors. Coins and tokens that capitalize on technological advancements or address specific market needs tend to attract investor interest and experience rapid price increases. As 2025 approaches, investors should closely monitor new projects and evaluate their fundamentals, especially in sectors such as decentralized finance (DeFi) and eco-friendly cryptocurrencies, which are gaining traction among ethical investors. Recognizing these trends early can lead to significant gains and a robust portfolio.

Furthermore, the rise of decentralized finance has reshaped traditional financial services, providing new avenues for investment and income generation. DeFi projects have gained popularity for their potential to offer higher returns compared to conventional banking options. Investors looking to participate should remain vigilant, as the landscape is constantly evolving, with new platforms and technologies emerging regularly. By understanding historical market trends related to DeFi, investors can better gauge the longevity and viability of these projects, ensuring they are aligned with their investment strategies.

Lastly, effective risk management remains a crucial component of any successful investment strategy in the cryptocurrency realm. Historical data indicates that price corrections are common, and understanding the cyclical nature of the market can help investors prepare for potential downturns. Employing techniques such as diversification and setting stop-loss orders are essential practices that can mitigate risks. With the insights gained from past market behavior, investors can develop a more nuanced approach to trading and investing in cryptocurrencies, ultimately enhancing their chances of success in the dynamic environment of 2025.

Predictions from Industry Experts

Predictions from industry experts regarding the cryptocurrency landscape in 2025 provide valuable insights for investors and day traders seeking to navigate this dynamic market. Analysts emphasize that the top cryptocurrencies, such as Bitcoin and Ethereum, are likely to maintain their dominance, yet emerging cryptocurrencies with innovative technologies and real-world applications are predicted to capture significant attention. Experts highlight that projects focusing on scalability, interoperability, and user experience will be crucial in attracting new investors and gaining market share. As such, investors should remain vigilant in identifying these high-growth potential cryptocurrencies that could redefine the market landscape.

Sustainable and eco-friendly cryptocurrencies are increasingly becoming a focal point for ethical investors. Industry experts forecast a surge in projects that prioritize environmental responsibility, driven by the growing global emphasis on sustainability. Cryptocurrencies that employ proof-of-stake mechanisms or other energy-efficient consensus algorithms are expected to gain traction. This shift not only aligns with ethical investing trends but also addresses regulatory pressures surrounding energy consumption in the crypto space. Investors are encouraged to consider these sustainable options as they diversify their portfolios and seek to align their investments with their values.

Decentralized Finance (DeFi) projects are poised for remarkable growth in 2025, according to industry specialists. As traditional financial systems grapple with inefficiencies, DeFi platforms offering innovative solutions for lending, borrowing, and trading are expected to attract a larger user base. Experts point out that successful DeFi projects will likely incorporate robust security measures and user-friendly interfaces, making them accessible to a wider audience. Investors should keep a close eye on emerging DeFi protocols that demonstrate strong fundamentals and community support, as these may represent lucrative investment opportunities in the evolving landscape.

As cryptocurrency markets mature, effective investment strategies become essential for both beginners and seasoned traders. Experts recommend a balanced approach that combines long-term holding with active trading strategies to capitalize on market fluctuations. Understanding risk management techniques is vital, as the volatility inherent in crypto markets can lead to significant losses. Investors are urged to establish clear entry and exit points, utilize stop-loss orders, and stay informed about market trends to mitigate risks. Furthermore, diversifying portfolios across various cryptocurrencies can help spread risk and enhance potential returns.

Market analysts predict that 2025 will bring an increased focus on NFTs (Non-Fungible Tokens) and their applications beyond digital art and collectibles. Experts suggest that investors should look for promising NFT projects that offer utility, community engagement, and innovative use cases. The growing intersection of NFTs with gaming, virtual reality, and metaverse applications is expected to drive demand and interest. Understanding the evolving landscape of NFTs will be critical for investors seeking to capitalize on this trend while also navigating the tax implications and regulatory considerations that accompany cryptocurrency investments.

Utilizing Data for Investment Decisions

Utilizing data effectively can be a game changer for cryptocurrency investors and day traders aiming to navigate the volatile landscape of digital currencies in 2025. In an era where information is abundant, distinguishing between useful data and noise is critical. Investors should focus on quantitative metrics such as price trends, trading volumes, market capitalization, and volatility indicators. Tools like technical analysis can help identify patterns in price movements, allowing traders to make informed decisions based on historical performance and potential future outcomes. Understanding these data points is essential for formulating both long-term and short-term investment strategies.

Emerging cryptocurrencies with high growth potential often exhibit unique data patterns that can signal investment opportunities. By analyzing whitepapers, team backgrounds, and project roadmaps, investors can assess the credibility and feasibility of new projects. Metrics such as user adoption rates and transaction volumes provide insight into market interest and usability. Moreover, keeping an eye on social media chatter and community engagement can offer qualitative data that amplifies quantitative findings. This multifaceted approach is crucial for identifying promising projects before they gain mainstream traction.

Sustainable and eco-friendly cryptocurrencies are increasingly appealing to ethical investors, especially as the conversation around climate change intensifies. Data on energy consumption and carbon footprints associated with different blockchain networks can guide investors toward projects that align with their values. Moreover, analyzing partnerships with environmental organizations or initiatives that promote sustainability can provide additional context. Investors should prioritize platforms that not only aim for profitability but also contribute positively to the environment, ensuring their investments resonate with their ethical considerations.

Decentralized Finance (DeFi) projects are another area ripe for data-driven investment strategies. The rapid growth of DeFi has led to a plethora of options, each with varying degrees of risk and reward. Investors should analyze key performance indicators such as total value locked (TVL) in protocols, liquidity pool sizes, and yield farming returns. Understanding the underlying mechanics of these projects through data analysis enables investors to identify which DeFi solutions are poised for stability and growth, providing a robust foundation for investment decisions.

As cryptocurrency markets evolve, so do the strategies for risk management. Utilizing data to establish risk tolerance levels and diversify portfolios is essential for mitigating potential losses. Investors should analyze correlations between different cryptocurrencies to optimize their asset allocation. This ensures that a downturn in one asset does not disproportionately affect the overall portfolio. Furthermore, staying informed on regulatory changes and market sentiment through data analysis can help investors adapt their strategies promptly, thereby enhancing their resilience in the face of market fluctuations.

Chapter 10: Diversifying Your Crypto Portfolio

Importance of Diversification

Diversification is a crucial strategy for anyone involved in the volatile world of cryptocurrency. In 2025, as emerging technologies and market dynamics shape the landscape, a well-diversified portfolio can help mitigate risks while maximizing potential returns. By spreading investments across different cryptocurrencies, investors can shield themselves from the adverse effects of price fluctuations that often plague individual assets. This approach not only enhances stability but also positions investors to capitalize on various growth opportunities that arise within the crypto market.

In the context of the top cryptocurrencies and emerging players, diversification allows investors to balance their exposure to established coins like Bitcoin and Ethereum with the potential high-growth assets that are gaining traction. As new projects enter the market, identifying those with strong fundamentals and innovative technology becomes vital. By allocating a portion of their portfolio to these emerging cryptocurrencies, investors can tap into the potential for significant returns while reducing the risk associated with concentrating too heavily on a single asset or sector.

For ethical investors, the rise of sustainable and eco-friendly cryptocurrencies presents yet another avenue for diversification. Investing in projects that prioritize environmental sustainability not only aligns with ethical considerations but also caters to a growing market demand for green technologies. By including these assets in their portfolios, investors can support initiatives that contribute positively to the planet while potentially benefiting from the increasing interest in eco-conscious investments.

DeFi projects represent another key area where diversification can yield significant advantages. As decentralized finance continues to revolutionize how we view traditional financial systems, investors have the opportunity to engage with various DeFi tokens that offer unique services and functionalities. By diversifying into different DeFi projects, investors can spread their risk across various platforms and use cases, ensuring they are not overly reliant on the success of any single protocol while accessing the potential high yields and innovative financial products that the DeFi space offers.

Finally, effective diversification should also encompass risk management techniques and an understanding of market trends. Investors must remain vigilant in analyzing market data and trends to make informed decisions about reallocating their portfolios. By regularly assessing the performance of their investments and adjusting their strategies accordingly, they can maintain a well-balanced portfolio that aligns with their risk tolerance and investment goals. This proactive approach allows investors to navigate the complexities of the crypto market while positioning themselves for sustainable growth in 2025 and beyond.

Strategies for a Balanced Portfolio

Creating a balanced cryptocurrency portfolio in 2025 requires a multifaceted approach that takes into account both established players and emerging assets. Investors should start by allocating a portion of their capital to top cryptocurrencies with a strong market presence, such as Bitcoin and Ethereum. These currencies have proven their resilience and offer a certain level of stability amidst the volatility that characterizes the crypto market. By ensuring a foundational investment in these well-established assets, investors can mitigate risks while allowing for growth as they explore other opportunities.

Incorporating emerging cryptocurrencies with high growth potential is crucial for a well-rounded portfolio. Projects that focus on innovative technology, real-world applications, or unique value propositions can yield significant returns. Conducting thorough research into the development teams, use cases, and market trends for these emerging assets is essential. Investors should look for tokens that address existing problems within the blockchain ecosystem or that have garnered community support. This exploration may lead to identifying the next big player in the market, akin to how early investors capitalized on Ethereum's rise.

Sustainable and eco-friendly cryptocurrencies are becoming increasingly important for ethical investors. As environmental concerns gain traction, many projects are focusing on reducing their carbon footprints. Investors should consider allocating a portion of their portfolio to these sustainable assets, which not only align with ethical investment principles but may also benefit from growing public interest and institutional backing. This strategy helps diversify the portfolio while supporting initiatives that prioritize environmental responsibility, creating a win-win scenario for both investors and the planet.

Risk management techniques are vital for anyone engaging in cryptocurrency trading, particularly for day traders who face market fluctuations daily. Employing strategies such as stop-loss orders, position sizing, and regular portfolio reviews can help minimize potential losses. Diversifying across various asset classes within the crypto space—such as DeFi projects and NFTs—can also reduce risk exposure. By spreading investments across multiple sectors, traders can cushion their portfolios against the adverse effects of market downturns in any single asset.

Finally, understanding the tax implications of cryptocurrency investments is essential for effective portfolio management. Investors should familiarize themselves with the regulations in their jurisdiction and maintain accurate records of their trades and holdings. Implementing strategies for capital gains tax management, such as tax-loss harvesting, can enhance overall returns. Balancing long-term and short-term investments further aids in tax efficiency, allowing investors to navigate the complexities of the crypto landscape while maximizing their financial outcomes.

Tools for Portfolio Management

In the rapidly evolving landscape of cryptocurrency investment, effective portfolio management is crucial for achieving long-term success. Investors can utilize a variety of tools to track, analyze, and optimize their digital asset holdings. Portfolio management tools help streamline the process of monitoring performance, assessing risk, and making informed decisions based on real-time market data.

As we approach 2025, understanding these tools becomes increasingly important for both novice and seasoned investors who are navigating the complexities of cryptocurrencies.

One of the most popular tools among cryptocurrency investors is portfolio tracking software. These applications allow users to input their various holdings and track their performance over time. Many tracking tools provide features such as price alerts, performance analytics, and profit-loss calculations. Some platforms even integrate with exchanges, enabling automatic updates of asset values. By utilizing these tools, investors can assess which cryptocurrencies are performing well and which may need to be reevaluated, ensuring a well-balanced and profitable portfolio.

In addition to tracking software, analytics platforms play a significant role in portfolio management. These tools offer in-depth market analysis, including historical price trends, trading volumes, and other essential metrics that can impact investment decisions. By analyzing data from multiple sources, investors can identify emerging cryptocurrencies with high growth potential, making informed decisions that align with their investment strategies. Advanced analytics tools also facilitate the exploration of DeFi projects and NFT opportunities, which are expected to gain traction in 2025.

Risk management is another critical aspect of effective portfolio management. Tools that focus on risk assessment and mitigation can help investors understand the volatility of their assets and the potential impact on their overall portfolio. Techniques such as diversification, stop-loss orders, and position sizing can be effectively managed with the right tools. By incorporating risk management tools, investors can protect their capital while still pursuing high-reward opportunities within the cryptocurrency market.

Lastly, tax management tools are increasingly important for crypto investors in 2025. As regulations surrounding cryptocurrency transactions tighten, understanding the tax implications of trading and investing becomes essential. These tools assist investors in tracking capital gains, calculating tax liabilities, and ensuring compliance with applicable laws. By integrating tax considerations into their portfolio management strategy, investors can maximize their returns while minimizing potential legal issues. Overall, leveraging these tools can significantly enhance an investor's ability to navigate the dynamic world of cryptocurrency effectively.

Chapter 11: Tax Implications and Strategies for Cryptocurrency Investors

Understanding Cryptocurrency Taxation

Understanding Cryptocurrency Taxation is essential for any investor navigating the rapidly evolving landscape of digital currencies. As cryptocurrencies gain popularity, the need for clarity regarding their tax implications has become increasingly important. Cryptocurrency is often treated as property by tax authorities in many jurisdictions, meaning that transactions involving cryptocurrencies can trigger capital gains tax liabilities. Investors must be aware that every trade, sale, or transfer of cryptocurrency can potentially have tax consequences, necessitating meticulous record-keeping and reporting.

In 2025, as new cryptocurrencies emerge and existing ones gain traction, understanding how each transaction affects your tax situation will be crucial. For instance, selling a portion of your holdings for profit, exchanging one cryptocurrency for another, or even using crypto to purchase goods can all result in taxable events. Investors should familiarize themselves with the specific regulations in their country regarding the treatment of cryptocurrency, as these rules can vary widely. This knowledge can help investors make informed decisions about when to buy, sell, or hold their assets.

Tax implications can also differ significantly based on the holding period of an investment. Long-term capital gains, typically applied to assets held for over a year, may be taxed at a lower rate compared to short-term gains. For cryptocurrency investors, this distinction can significantly impact overall tax liabilities. Strategies focusing on long-term investment can not only align with a more sustainable investment approach but also provide potential tax benefits. Understanding these nuances can help investors plan their strategies more effectively.

Additionally, as the cryptocurrency market continues to diversify with emerging projects and DeFi platforms, investors should be aware of how income generated from these sources is taxed. Yield farming, staking, and earning interest on crypto holdings can all introduce different tax reporting requirements. Investors engaged in these activities should stay informed about how their activities may be classified and the implications for their annual tax filings. Seeking advice from tax professionals who specialize in cryptocurrency can be invaluable in navigating these complexities.

Finally, effective risk management strategies in cryptocurrency trading should encompass tax considerations. Investors should not only focus on minimizing losses through market strategies but also consider how their trading activities will impact their tax obligations. By incorporating tax planning into their overall investment strategy, crypto investors can optimize their portfolios while staying compliant with the law. Understanding cryptocurrency taxation is not merely a compliance issue; it is a critical component of a comprehensive investment strategy that can enhance overall returns and reduce unexpected liabilities.

Reporting Requirements for Investors

Reporting requirements for investors in the cryptocurrency space are becoming increasingly important as regulatory bodies around the world tighten their grip on this rapidly evolving market. Investors must be aware of their obligations regarding reporting income and transactions related to their cryptocurrency investments. This subchapter will outline the essential reporting requirements that cryptocurrency investors, including day traders and long-term holders, should consider to remain compliant and avoid potential penalties.

Primarily, cryptocurrency investors need to understand that the Internal Revenue Service (IRS) treats cryptocurrencies as property for tax purposes. This classification means that any gains or losses from trading cryptocurrencies are subject to capital gains tax. Consequently, investors must keep meticulous records of their transactions, including the date of acquisition, the value at the time of purchase, and the date and value at the time of sale. This detailed documentation is crucial for accurately calculating taxable gains and losses, especially for those engaging in frequent trading or holding multiple cryptocurrencies.

In addition to capital gains reporting, investors should also be aware of income generated through cryptocurrency activities, such as staking, lending, or participating in Initial Coin Offerings (ICOs). Any income received in the form of cryptocurrency must be reported as ordinary income based on its fair market value at the time of receipt. This requirement applies to both individual investors and those operating as businesses in the cryptocurrency sector. Understanding these distinctions is fundamental to ensuring compliance with tax regulations.

As the cryptocurrency landscape continues to evolve, emerging regulations may impose additional reporting requirements, such as the need to disclose foreign accounts holding cryptocurrencies or transactions exceeding certain thresholds. Investors should stay informed about potential changes in legislation that could affect their reporting obligations. Engaging with knowledgeable tax professionals who specialize in cryptocurrency can provide valuable insights and help investors navigate the complexities of compliance.

Lastly, the importance of transparent reporting cannot be overstated, especially for investors interested in sustainable and eco-friendly cryptocurrencies or decentralized finance (DeFi) projects. Adhering to reporting requirements not only protects investors from legal repercussions but also fosters trust within the broader cryptocurrency ecosystem. By maintaining high standards of compliance, investors contribute to the legitimacy and acceptance of cryptocurrencies in mainstream financial markets, ultimately benefiting their portfolios and the industry as a whole.

Tax-Efficient Investment Strategies

Tax-efficient investment strategies are essential for cryptocurrency investors looking to maximize their returns while minimizing their tax liabilities. In the rapidly evolving landscape of crypto assets, understanding the tax implications of various investment approaches can significantly impact overall profitability. Crypto investors must navigate complex tax regulations, which vary by jurisdiction and can change frequently. Therefore, staying informed about these regulations and employing tax-efficient strategies can be vital for optimizing investment outcomes.

One effective strategy for tax efficiency is the use of long-term holding or "HODLing." By holding cryptocurrencies for more than a year before selling, investors may qualify for lower long-term capital gains tax rates. This approach not only reduces tax liabilities but also aligns with the inherent volatility of crypto markets. Many successful investors have capitalized on the long-term growth potential of established cryptocurrencies like Bitcoin and Ethereum, benefiting from the appreciation in value while deferring tax payments until they decide to sell.

In addition to long-term holding, tax-loss harvesting is a strategy that can help offset gains with losses. Investors can sell underperforming assets at a loss to reduce their taxable income, thereby lowering their overall tax burden. This strategy is particularly relevant in the highly volatile crypto market, where price fluctuations can lead to both gains and losses. By strategically selling assets that have depreciated, investors can create a more favorable tax position while potentially reinvesting in more promising projects.

Another important aspect of tax-efficient investing is the consideration of tax-advantaged accounts. Some jurisdictions allow for the use of Individual Retirement Accounts (IRAs) or similar vehicles to invest in cryptocurrencies. These accounts can provide significant tax benefits, such as tax deferral on earnings or tax-free withdrawals in retirement. Investors should explore these options to enhance their tax efficiency and secure their financial future while engaging in cryptocurrency investments.

Finally, it is crucial for investors to maintain meticulous records of all transactions, including purchases, sales, and exchanges of cryptocurrencies. Keeping accurate records allows investors to calculate gains and losses accurately and ensures compliance with tax regulations. Utilizing accounting software or hiring a tax professional familiar with cryptocurrency can aid in managing this complex process. By implementing these tax-efficient strategies, cryptocurrency investors can position themselves for greater financial success while navigating the intricacies of tax obligations in the crypto landscape.

Chapter 12: Long-Term vs. Short-Term Investment Strategies in Crypto

Defining Investment Horizons

Defining an investment horizon is crucial for any cryptocurrency investor, as it influences decision-making, risk tolerance, and overall strategy. In the rapidly evolving landscape of cryptocurrencies, the time frame for which one intends to hold an asset can vary greatly, impacting both the potential returns and the level of volatility one is willing to endure. Investors must recognize that different cryptocurrencies may serve distinct purposes within their portfolios, whether they are viewed as long-term holds, short-term trading opportunities, or speculative plays. Understanding these time frames enables investors to align their strategies with their financial goals and risk profiles.

For beginners, distinguishing between short-term and long-term investment horizons is particularly important. Short-term traders often engage in day trading or swing trading, capitalizing on market fluctuations to achieve quick gains. This approach requires a keen awareness of market trends, technical analysis, and risk management techniques to navigate the inherent volatility of the crypto space. Conversely, long-term investors may focus on established cryptocurrencies or emerging projects with solid fundamentals, aiming to benefit from the potential appreciation over several years. By defining their investment horizon, traders and investors can tailor their research and strategy to maximize their chances of success.

In 2025, the landscape of cryptocurrencies is likely to be influenced by emerging trends, including the rise of decentralized finance (DeFi) and sustainable cryptocurrencies. Investors should consider how these trends fit into their investment horizons. For instance, DeFi projects may offer high growth potential for those with a willingness to engage in more active trading strategies, while sustainable cryptocurrencies may attract long-term investors who prioritize ethical considerations alongside financial performance. The decision to invest in these niches should reflect an investor's time frame and risk appetite, as well as their commitment to specific values in the crypto space.

Risk management is another critical aspect tied to investment horizons. Short-term traders must implement rigorous risk management techniques, including stop-loss orders and position sizing, to protect their capital from sudden market downturns. Long-term investors, on the other hand, may adopt a more patient approach, focusing on the fundamental strengths of their chosen assets. However, even long-term investors need to remain vigilant and adaptable to market changes, as the cryptocurrency market is notorious for its rapid shifts in sentiment and value. By understanding the implications of their investment horizons, investors can better navigate these risks.

Ultimately, defining investment horizons is a strategic exercise that can significantly influence the outcomes of cryptocurrency investments. Whether engaging in day trading, venturing into emerging altcoins, or holding sustainable assets for the long haul, investors must remain aligned with their financial goals and risk tolerance. As the crypto market continues to evolve, those who take the time to assess and define their investment horizons will be better positioned to capitalize on opportunities and mitigate risks, paving the way for success in the dynamic environment of cryptocurrency investing in 2025 and beyond.

Pros and Cons of Each Strategy

When analyzing the various strategies for investing in cryptocurrencies, it is essential to weigh the pros and cons of each approach to determine what aligns best with individual financial goals and risk appetites. Long-term investment strategies, often appealing to those who believe in the sustained growth of specific cryptocurrencies, offer the advantage of lower transaction costs and a reduced need for constant market monitoring. Investors can benefit from compounding returns and the potential resilience of well-established currencies like Bitcoin and Ethereum. However, the downside includes exposure to market volatility over extended periods, which can lead to significant drawdowns that test the patience and mental fortitude of investors.

Conversely, short-term investment strategies, such as day trading, have gained popularity due to their potential for quick returns. Day traders can capitalize on market fluctuations, employing technical analysis to make rapid buy and sell decisions. This approach can lead to substantial profits in a bullish market, but it also carries significant risks. High transaction fees, the requirement for constant market monitoring, and the emotional toll of rapid trading can deter many from this strategy. Additionally, the unpredictability of short-term price movements means that losses can accumulate quickly, making risk management techniques crucial for anyone engaging in this approach.

Emerging cryptocurrencies present another avenue for investors looking to maximize returns in 2025. These lesser-known assets often come with high growth potential, appealing to those willing to take calculated risks. Early investment in promising projects can yield impressive returns if the cryptocurrency gains traction. However, the high volatility and lack of historical data on these assets can lead to uncertainty. Investors must conduct thorough research to avoid pitfalls associated with scams or projects lacking real utility, making due diligence essential for mitigating risks.

Sustainable and eco-friendly cryptocurrencies are gaining traction among ethical investors who prioritize environmental considerations. These assets often promote reduced energy consumption and contribute to sustainability goals. The appeal lies in aligning investments with personal values while still seeking financial returns. Nevertheless, these projects might face challenges in terms of market adoption and competition from more established cryptocurrencies that do not prioritize eco-friendliness. As the market evolves, balancing ethical considerations with financial viability will be key for investors in this niche.

Finally, decentralized finance (DeFi) projects offer innovative opportunities for investment and engagement in the crypto space. These platforms allow users to lend, borrow, and trade without traditional intermediaries, fostering financial inclusion and accessibility. The potential for high yields in DeFi protocols can be enticing, but investors must also consider the risks involved, such as smart contract vulnerabilities and regulatory uncertainties. Understanding these dynamics is critical for navigating the rapidly changing landscape of DeFi and making informed investment decisions. A comprehensive approach to analyzing these strategies can empower investors to build robust portfolios that align with their financial objectives and risk tolerance.

Creating a Hybrid Approach

As the cryptocurrency landscape continues to evolve, investors are recognizing the need for a hybrid investment strategy that combines various methodologies to maximize returns while mitigating risks. This approach integrates long-term investments in established cryptocurrencies with short-term trading strategies in emerging assets. By balancing these two styles, investors can capitalize on the volatility of the market while holding onto stable coins or blue-chip cryptocurrencies to ensure a safety net in their portfolios.

Emerging cryptocurrencies with high growth potential represent a critical component of this hybrid strategy. In 2025, numerous new projects are expected to enter the market, offering innovative solutions and addressing real-world problems. Investors should focus on conducting thorough research to identify these promising assets early on. Engaging with communities, analyzing project roadmaps, and understanding the technology behind these cryptocurrencies can provide insights that lead to significant gains. By integrating these high-risk, high-reward investments with a stable core of established currencies, investors can position themselves for growth while maintaining a safety margin.

Sustainable and eco-friendly cryptocurrencies are also gaining traction among ethical investors. This niche is particularly relevant as environmental concerns continue to shape public perception and regulatory frameworks surrounding blockchain technology. Investors can create a hybrid portfolio that includes both traditional cryptocurrencies and green alternatives, allowing them to support initiatives that prioritize sustainability. By investing in projects that utilize proof-of-stake mechanisms or other energy-efficient protocols, investors can align their financial goals with their values, enhancing the long-term viability of their portfolios.

Decentralized Finance (DeFi) projects are another critical aspect of a successful hybrid approach in 2025. These platforms offer innovative financial services without intermediaries, providing opportunities for yield farming, lending, and staking. However, they also come with unique risks that require careful management. Investors should consider diversifying their holdings within the DeFi space while employing risk management techniques to safeguard their investments. This might include setting stop-loss orders, allocating a specific percentage of their portfolio to DeFi assets, and continuously monitoring market trends to make informed decisions.

In conclusion, a hybrid approach to cryptocurrency investment in 2025 allows investors to navigate the complexities of the market with greater agility and resilience. By integrating long-term holdings with short-term trading, focusing on emerging assets, and considering ethical investments, investors can create a balanced portfolio that is responsive to market dynamics. As they explore DeFi opportunities and employ effective risk management techniques, they will be better equipped to identify promising NFT projects and capitalize on trends, ultimately enhancing their potential for success in the ever-evolving crypto landscape.

Chapter 13: Conclusion and Future Outlook

Recap of Key Insights

In the rapidly evolving landscape of cryptocurrency, understanding the key insights that emerged throughout 2025 is crucial for investors and day traders alike. The year has witnessed a significant maturation of the market, with several cryptocurrencies establishing themselves as frontrunners. Bitcoin and Ethereum continue to dominate, but the rise of emerging currencies like Cardano and Solana showcases the potential for high growth in lesser-known assets. Investors should keep a keen eye on these developments, as they can lead to lucrative opportunities in the coming years.

Sustainable and eco-friendly cryptocurrencies have gained traction as ethical investing becomes more mainstream. Projects focused on reducing their carbon footprint and promoting environmental responsibility are not only appealing to socially conscious investors but also positioning themselves favorably in a market that increasingly values sustainability. Cryptocurrencies like Algorand and Chia are noteworthy examples, emphasizing the importance of aligning investment strategies with personal values and global trends.

DeFi projects have revolutionized the financial landscape, providing decentralized alternatives to traditional banking systems. The explosive growth of platforms like Uniswap and Aave highlights the potential for innovation within this sector. Investors should pay attention to new DeFi protocols emerging in 2025, as they often present unique opportunities for high returns and diversification. Understanding the mechanics of these platforms is essential for anyone looking to leverage DeFi's capabilities effectively.

Risk management remains a cornerstone of successful cryptocurrency trading. With market volatility presenting both challenges and opportunities, employing sound risk management techniques is vital. Strategies such as setting stop-loss orders, diversifying portfolios, and regularly assessing market conditions can mitigate potential losses. Beginners, in particular, should familiarize themselves with these techniques to navigate the complexities of the crypto market confidently.

Lastly, the NFT market continues to flourish, presenting new avenues for investment. Identifying promising NFT projects requires thorough research and an understanding of market trends. Investors should explore platforms that highlight unique digital assets, as these can yield substantial returns if chosen wisely. Additionally, a comprehensive approach to taxation and an awareness of the implications of cryptocurrency investments are essential for maintaining compliance and maximizing profits. Balancing long-term and short-term investment strategies will further enhance the potential for success in the dynamic world of cryptocurrency.

Looking Ahead: The Future of Crypto Investing

As we move into 2025, the landscape of crypto investing is set to evolve significantly. Investors can expect to see the emergence of new cryptocurrencies that promise high growth potential, fueled by advancements in technology and increasing adoption across various sectors. This year, potential winners may include projects focused on solving real-world problems, such as scalability and transaction speed, as well as those that cater to niche markets like gaming and digital identity verification. Being attuned to these developments will be crucial for investors looking to capitalize on early-stage opportunities.

Sustainability in crypto has gained traction, prompting a wave of eco-friendly cryptocurrencies designed to minimize environmental impact. Investors seeking ethical options will find a growing number of projects emphasizing green technologies and sustainable practices. These cryptocurrencies often utilize proof-of-stake or other energy-efficient consensus mechanisms that not only lower their carbon footprint but also enhance their appeal to socially conscious investors. As sustainability becomes a priority for more investors, those who align their portfolios with these values may find themselves ahead of the curve.

Decentralized Finance (DeFi) continues to be a robust area for investment, with numerous innovative projects on the horizon. In 2025, opportunities within DeFi will likely expand, providing investors with new avenues for yield generation and liquidity provision. Monitoring emerging DeFi protocols that are developing unique financial products can lead to potential high returns. Investors should familiarize themselves with the risks inherent in this space, including smart contract vulnerabilities and regulatory scrutiny, while also considering the long-term implications of these technologies on traditional finance.

For newcomers to the crypto market, understanding investment strategies and risk management techniques is essential for navigating its volatility. Educating oneself on the various approaches, whether long-term holding or day trading, can provide a solid foundation for making informed decisions. Diversification remains a key strategy, enabling investors to mitigate risks by spreading their capital across multiple assets. Additionally, being aware of tax implications and regulatory changes in the cryptocurrency space will help investors maintain compliance while optimizing their portfolios for maximum returns.

As market trends fluctuate, the ability to analyze market data and identify promising NFT projects will become increasingly important. Trends in digital art, gaming, and virtual real estate are likely to shape the NFT market in 2025, presenting unique investment opportunities. Investors should also pay close attention to the broader economic indicators that influence cryptocurrency prices, such as interest rates and geopolitical events. By staying informed and adaptable, investors can position themselves for success in the ever-changing world of cryptocurrency.

Final Thoughts for Investors

As we approach the conclusion of this exploration into the evolving landscape of cryptocurrency, it is vital for investors to reflect on the key lessons learned and consider their implications for the upcoming year. The rapid growth of the cryptocurrency market, combined with the emergence of new technologies and innovative projects, presents both opportunities and challenges. Investors should remain vigilant, continuously educating themselves about market trends and the unique characteristics of various cryptocurrencies. This knowledge will empower them to make informed decisions and adapt their strategies as necessary.

The importance of diversification cannot be overstated in the context of cryptocurrency investments. With the market being inherently volatile, spreading investments across different currencies and sectors can mitigate risks significantly. Investors should consider allocating portions of their portfolios to emerging cryptocurrencies with high growth potential, as well as sustainable and eco-friendly options that align with ethical investing principles. Additionally, maintaining a balanced approach that includes both DeFi projects and promising NFT initiatives can enhance overall portfolio resilience while capitalizing on new trends.

Risk management techniques are essential for navigating the unpredictable nature of the cryptocurrency market. Investors must develop a clear understanding of their risk tolerance and establish parameters for their investments. This could involve setting stop-loss orders, regularly reassessing positions, and keeping up with market news to remain agile in response to sudden changes. By implementing robust risk management strategies, investors can protect their capital while seeking opportunities for growth.

For those just starting in cryptocurrency, understanding investment strategies is crucial. Beginners should focus on foundational concepts, such as distinguishing between long-term and short-term investment strategies. Both approaches have their merits, and aligning them with personal financial goals and market conditions can optimize potential returns. Furthermore, it is essential to consider tax implications and strategies related to cryptocurrency investments. Staying informed about the regulatory landscape will ensure compliance and help investors navigate their tax responsibilities efficiently.

Finally, as we look forward to 2025, the importance of staying adaptable cannot be overemphasized. The cryptocurrency market is characterized by rapid change, and the ability to analyze market trends and predictions will be key for successful investing. Regularly assessing the performance of investments and being open to pivoting strategies will allow investors to seize new opportunities as they arise. By combining thorough research, sound investment principles, and a commitment to ongoing education, investors can position themselves for success in the dynamic world of cryptocurrency.

www.ingramcontent.com/pod-product-compliance
Lightning Source LLC
Chambersburg PA
CBHW070413230526
45471CB00006B/2785